I Want to Know™

About GOD

Rick Osborne and K. Christie Bowler

ZondervanPublishingHouse

Grand Rapids, Michigan

A Division of HarperCollins *Publishers*

20

For Lightwave
 Managing Editor: Elaine Osborne
 Art Director: Terry Van Roon

God copyright © 1998 by The Zondervan Corporation.

Artwork and Text copyright © 1998 by Lightwave Publishing Inc. All rights reserved.
http://www.lightwavepublishing.com

Scripture portions taken from the *Holy Bible, New International Reader's Version* Copyright © 1994, 1996 by International Bible Society.

Photos on pages 11, 18, 19, and 27 courtesy of Zondervan Publishing House.
Photo on page 8 courtesy of NASA.
The images used on pages 4, 5, 14, 16, 17, 18, and 25 were obtained from IMSI's Master Photo Collection, 1895 Francisco Blvd. East, San Rafael, CA 94901-5506, USA.

Library of Congress Cataloging-in-Publication Data

Osborne, Rick, 1961– .
  God / Rick Osborne and K. Christie Bowler.
    p. cm.—(I want to know™)
  Summary: Describes God and the various ways we can know about God, especially through Jesus.
  ISBN 0–310–22090–4
  1. God—Attributes—Juvenile literature. 2. God—Biblical teaching—Juvenile literature. [1. God. 2. Christian life.] I. Bowler, Christie, 1958– . II. Title. III. Series: Osborne, Rick, 1961– . I want to know™.
  BT130.083   1998
  231—dc21   98-9633
                                      CIP
                                      AC

This edition is printed on acid-free paper and meets the American National Standards Institute Z39.48 standard.

Published by Zondervan Publishing House, Grand Rapids, Michigan 49530, U.S.A. http://www.zondervan.com

Printed in Mexico.

LIGHTwave
Building Christian faith in families

A Lightwave Production
P.O. Box 160 Maple Ridge
B.C., Canada V2X 7G1

99 00 /DR/ 5 4 3

Contents

4

God the Creator

He Made It

Breathe deeply. Feel the air fill your lungs—air with the right proportions of the right gases to keep you alive. On a clear night, look up—millions of stars! Listen—frogs croak, crickets sing! Every part is important: stars, air, insects, tides. . . .

What makes galaxies spin? What causes insects to pollinate flowers at the right time? How do salt's two poisonous chemicals become something we can't live without? How did Earth become perfectly balanced, perfectly placed, perfectly inhabited? The questions are endless.

And the answer is God! He planned and created everything ideal for life. In fact, if any of thousands of details were different there would be no life! God made the immense universe with galaxies so huge we can't imagine them and atoms so small we'll probably never see them.

Creation is incredible! But not as incredible as its Creator!

He Cares

How can such an amazing God have time for us? Easy. We're why he made it all! We're front and center in his mind. If he takes care of life's details for his creatures, providing nests for birds, perfect beaks for hummingbirds to get nectar, and air bladders for fish to swim, he'll take care of us. We're more important to him than birds and fish!

God's creation shows us God. "Ever since the world was created it has been possible to see the qualities of God that are not seen. I'm talking about his eternal power and about the fact that he is God. Those things can be seen in what he has made" (Romans 1:20).

- *God loves balance.* Earth is the right distance from the sun to support life. Our atmosphere has the right proportions of gases.

- *He cares.* He provides everything that makes life possible. Plants turn the sun's light into food. Bacteria help us digest.

- *He keeps things in order.* God made the world work by rules to keep us safe—gravity makes things fall, light travels in straight lines.

- *He's trustworthy.* The HUGE universe and our small planet are in his hands.

- *No detail is too small for him.* Each creature is perfectly designed for its environment—hunting leopards blend into the trees, mussels' super-glue keeps them safe from waves.

- *He's intelligent.* We think and learn. It takes someone intelligent to make someone intelligent.

- *He gave us rest.* Creation goes in cycles—night/day, winter/summer, work/play.

In the beginning God created everything and put all the details in place. Creation makes it clear there is a God behind it all. Who is this God? What is he like? What does that have to do with us? Let's find out!

Desert Master

God specially engineered the one-hump dromedary for the desert. They're:

Perfectly Sand-Proof:
- Long eyelashes and inner eyelids keep sand out.

- Stretchy hooves prevent sinking.

- Nostrils close partway to keep out sand and let air in.

Perfect Water Users:
- Their eighty-pound hump is full of fat to use when there's no water.

- After losing 225 pounds in eight days without water, a ten-minute drink of twenty-seven gallons brings them back to normal.

- Blood reduces from 94 percent water to 60 percent without harm. (If our blood goes to 82 percent water, we die!)

God Is Real

How Do We Know God Is Real?

Have you ever seen, tasted, or smelled God? Is he real? Does it make sense to believe in God? Think about this: Have you ever tasted or smelled love? No. Is it real? Absolutely! We know love is real because we see what it does: kind acts, hugs, forgiveness, smiles, acceptance. In the same way, looking at what God has done helps us know God is real. That's why we can learn about him from what he made.

Think about these things and see if they don't help you know God is real.

He Designed It

Look around. Notice anything? Objects fall down. Trees grow up. With heat, water boils and wood burns. The sun rises every day. The world is predictable and orderly. It follows a design so well that scientists can make rules about it! Is this chance? Not likely! That's like saying the *Mona Lisa* painting was made by a paint spill. NOT! Just as someone painted Mona Lisa, someone designed the world: God.

He's the Source of...

Intelligence: You're reading this. You can think. Ever wonder how you do that? Thinking is complicated. Where did it come from? Someone thought up thinking and made the world an intelligent place. That someone is God, the first thinker and source of thinking.

The God idea: Throughout history people have believed in God or gods. Where did that idea come from? Why is it everywhere? God put it into us. He built us to know he's real!

Conscience: If you tell a lie or are mean, you probably feel bad. Your conscience tells you that you did something wrong. How do you know some things are right and others wrong? Your parents taught you some of it, but they couldn't give you a conscience. No, it came from the one who made right and wrong: God.

Beauty: We live in a beautiful world! Sunsets, flowers, faces, paintings, scenery. We enjoy beauty—think of our response to newborn kittens or rainbows. But beauty doesn't do anything. Something doesn't have to be beautiful to work. So why have it? Who would make something nice for no reason except enjoyment? God would!

"Foolish people say in their hearts, 'There is no God'" (Psalm 14:1). Think about it. Look around and ask questions about what you see, why it's there, or why it works the way it does.

Eventually your questions will lead you back to the ultimate answer: God. He's definitely real! He has to be for us to have a world to live in and think about.

Better and Best

Here's something to get your head around: Why do we think one thing is better than another? We think a multispeed mountain bike is better than a tricycle. A vacation is better than staying home. A poor but happy family is better than a lonely rich person. Where do we get the standard of better and best? No matter what we think of, we can usually think of something better. But eventually, somewhere there has to be an ultimate BEST that beats out everything else. Somewhere there is something or someone that *nothing* can be better than: God.

God Is Awesome

He's Everywhere

God is real. He has always been and always will be. We know he's spirit (he has no physical body), but what's he *like?* Can we know? Yes! Nature teaches general things about God. But God wants us to know him in detail. He gave us a book, the Bible, that tells us what he's like, how life works, and more.

Look in the mirror. You're not a shapeless blob oozing out into endless space. You have limits; you fill a certain space and have edges separating you from your surroundings. Everything has limits. Except God. The Bible tells us God is *omnipresent*—present everywhere. He fills the universe. Go anywhere—God is already there! "Who can hide in secret places so that I can't see them?. . . Don't I fill heaven and earth?" (Jeremiah 23:24).

He Knows Everything

You know things and you learn more every day, at school and at home. Everyone learns. Not God. He's *omniscient*—he already knows everything, from what you like for breakfast, to how to make a planet, to what unborn people will do.

Everywhere you go your knowledge goes. You can't take out bits, like how to add, and stick them in the hamper with your dirty shirts. They're part of you. God can't be somewhere without his knowledge either. Everything he knows is everywhere he is.

"The Lord knows what people think. . . . There is no limit to his understanding. . . . He even counts every hair on your head! . . . Nothing God created is hidden from him. His eyes see everything" (Psalm 94:11; 147:5; Matthew 10:29–30; Hebrews 4:13).

He Can Do Anything

Can you do whatever you want? Can you fly or breathe under water? Nope. You don't have the power. In fact, you can't even make yourself taller! But God can do *anything* and *everything* he wants. He's *omnipotent*—all-powerful. He spoke and the universe was created! "Great is our Lord. His power is mighty. . . . You have made the heavens and the earth. Nothing is too hard for you. . . . With people that is impossible. But with God, all things are possible" (Psalm 147:5; Jeremiah 32:17; Matthew 19:26).

It Affects Us

We have limits: stops and starts, beginnings and ends. But God doesn't. That's great! You see, who God is affects us. Because he's everywhere, we're never alone. Because he can do anything, he can help with any problem. Because he knows everything, including what's best for us, he can give us perfect advice. God told us these things about himself so we'd know we can trust him.

A Hamster-Eye View

Two hamsters look outside their cage and argue about whether what they see (you) is real. They can't touch or understand you—you're so much bigger than they are—so they decide you're not real. Silly, huh? They decide what's real by their understanding and experience. But they don't have all the information to make a good decision. Even if they did, it wouldn't make sense to them. But no matter what they do or don't know, you're still real.

Like hamsters, we don't have all the information about God. And some of what we do know is hard to understand. But it would be silly to decide God can't be real just because we can't figure him out!

The Only God

The One and Only

There are no other gods besides God. Think about it: If you made a whole village out of play dough, would there be things in it you didn't make? No way. In the same way, since God made everything in the uni-verse, it's impossible for creation to contain anything God didn't make. So there can't be some other "god" out there somewhere. Besides, if God fills every-thing (which he does), where would other "gods" live? There's no place for them.

"I am the one and only God. Before me, there was no other god at all. And there will not be any god after me. . . . I am the First and the Last. I am the one and only God. . . . There is no other god" (Isaiah 43:10; 44:6; 46:9).

Three in One

One bike. What happens if you take the bike apart? No more bike—only parts of a bike. One means a whole. God is one. You can't divide him into parts. Everything God is, he is all the time. His qualities, like omnipres-ence, are part of his *nature*, they make him who he is. At the same time, the Bible says God is three! Look at Jesus' baptism (Matthew 3:16–17). Jesus the *Son* was in the water. The *Spirit* came down like a dove. And the *Father* spoke from heaven. God is three persons—Father, Son, and Holy Spirit. God is all three at the same time, and they're all one God! They're not parts of God. All three share the same nature—they all fill everything, know everything, and can do everything. Therefore they're one God. So what makes them three? Their persons and their jobs.

Think about it like this: Imagine your best friend and you have no bodies. You both fill everything (including each other). You both know everything (including each other's thoughts), and you both can do anything. In almost every way you and your friend would be the same—two-in-one. Only two things would make you different from each other: your personalities and what you decided together you would each look after or be responsible for. You would be two persons sharing one nature.

Three Persons, Three Jobs

The Father: Source and creator of everything. "He is the Father. All things come from him" (1 Corinthians 8:6). He sent his Son. Jesus said, "The Father who sent me. . ." (John 5:37).

The Son, Jesus Christ: Died to save us from our sins. "While we were still sinners, Christ died for us" (Romans 5:8). He will judge us. "The Father . . . has given the Son the task of judging" (John 5:22). He prays for us. "Christ Jesus is . . . praying for us" (Romans 8:34).

The Holy Spirit: He's with us. "[God] will give you another Friend to help you and to be with you forever. The Friend is the Spirit of truth" (John 14:16–17). He helps, teaches, and grows us to be more like Jesus. "He will teach you all things. He will remind you of everything I have said to you" (John 14:26). "Salvation comes through the Holy Spirit's work. He makes people holy" (2 Thessalonians 2:13). He gives us gifts. "Different kinds of gifts . . . are all given by the same Spirit" (1 Corinthians 12:4).

The dove is a symbol of the Holy Spirit.

People use different pictures to understand how God is three in one.

He Made Us

Made by the Best

God made everything. But why make us?

Say you're alive forever and can do absolutely anything. What would it be? Fly around for ninety years? Play ball for sixty? Seriously, how would you spend your time? God must have thought about it because he decided to do something incredible! He made the universe, filled it with galaxies, planets, stars, and black holes. Then he made life on Earth. He made all kinds of living things: microscopic critters, maple trees, crabs, dolphins, puppy dogs and ants, lions and kangaroos. He made oceans, mountains, rivers, deserts, and forests. He made everything around us. Then he made something different from everything else: people!

Have you ever wondered what makes you different from your pet dog, gerbil, or fish? Well, you talk. You wear clothes, ride a bike, and go to school. But the real difference is in how we were made.

Made Like the Best

God, the Best, made us like himself—like God! We're made in his *image*. God is different from us, true, but in some ways we're like him:

God is spirit: We have spirits. Our spirit makes us alive. A body without a spirit is just skin and bones. Our spirits will live forever with God when this life is over.

God knows and God does: Like God, we have minds that let us learn and know things. We think and plan. We have wills that let us choose. We act and make things happen.

God is in charge of everything he made: He's responsible and does what he promises. He gave us responsibilities too—to take care of the world and each other.

God has emotions: He feels love, anger, grief, and joy. Like God, we get upset or feel joy. We laugh at a good joke or just because. We love our family and friends, and we feel their love for us.

Children of the Best

Why did God interrupt his peaceful existence to make the universe? Why make you and me? Because he wanted someone to love, and he wanted to be loved by us. God wanted a family, so the Father, Son, and Spirit made a family of humans. The plan was that God would pour out all his love onto this human family, and we would pour out our love on him. We would love him, obey him out of trust, enjoy his company, and receive his incredible love.

God wanted to care for us, protect us, guide us, teach us, and help us be more like him so that we can be the best possible people and have the best possible lives. He made us because he is love. He planned for us to be together as the best and closest family ever. "Father, I pray that all of them will be one, just as you are in me and I am in you. I want them also to be in us" (John 17:21). "How great is the love the Father has given us so freely! Now we can be called children of God. And that's what we really are!" (1 John 3:1).

God created everything. Can you find Adam and Eve, the first people? How many animals are in the picture?

We Chose Poorly

A Bad Choice

This Father/child relationship with God sounds great! What happened? The first people ruined it!

Say you have a pile of fruit to choose from. God tells you the orange striped one will kill you and change the world forever. No orange striped fruit for you! But what if someone says, "Aw, it won't kill you. It'll make you really smart!" Now what? Just a nibble? That's what happened to the first people, Adam and Eve. They ate the forbidden fruit and wrecked everything.

Why did God let them? He loved them. He wanted their love to be given back freely. That means Adam and Eve had to be able to choose *not* to love God. And that's what they did. They didn't trust him. They went their own way, which is sin, instead of trusting God's love. That choice ruined the relationship for everyone who came after them. Bad choice!

Homeless

Imagine running away from home: Nowhere to sleep. No food or shelter. Did your parents want you to be cold and hungry? No. Your parents want to care and provide for you. *You* made the choice to run away.

God wants the best for us too. That best means being part of his family. He wants to care for us and make sure we have everything we need and then some. His plan is to love us as his children. But we (through Adam and Eve) ran away from home.

Made for Family

God created relationships as a wonderful blessing in our lives—relationships with him and with each other. "God said, 'It is not good for the man to be alone. I will make a helper who is just right for him'" (Genesis 2:18). We were made for family. That's God's gift to us.

Some may think it's not fair that God made us need him. That's like saying it's not fair that we have to eat. Was God mean to make us need food? Of course not. In fact, he made food wonderful! God made chewy pizza and mouth-watering chocolate.

He made food to bless us.

That's how relationships should be—a pleasure. God made us to need him and each other because it's good for us. Loneliness was never in the plan. Friendships make life good. But a good relationship with God makes it even better! Adam and Eve wrecked their relationship with God when they chose sin. To get back into God's family, we have to return to God.

Satan, disguised as a snake, told Eve the fruit would make her like God.

Adam and Eve disobeyed God and ate the fruit.

Consequences and Judgment

CRASH! One broken vase. And one big punishment! Why do your parents discipline you? They're trying to help you become wise and mature. They forgive you, but there are consequences: you pay for the vase. The world works by consequences: play with fire and you get burned; lie and people will stop trusting you.

God made the world to work in certain ways that match who he is. When we trust God and do things his way, life works better. When we don't do them his way and sin instead, things go wrong. Sin has consequences.

God doesn't want to be our judge. He wants to be our Father. He corrects and teaches us for our sake.

Results of the Fall

Lies and Rumors

Ever since Adam and Eve chose not to have a relationship with God, people have gotten wrong and weird ideas about what God is like and who he is. They began to think he was different than he was. They stopped believing he was a loving Father. Satan (who told Adam and Eve God was wrong and the fruit wouldn't hurt them) spread lies about God.

When a relationship breaks, we no longer know the other person well. It's easy to believe lies about them.

Wrong Thoughts of God

It wasn't long before people were making up untrue things about God and how the world works. They started believing the lies and teaching them as if they were true. **But** in the Bible, God tells us the truth about the world and himself. Take a look at these false beliefs about God. Then look at what God says:

Agnosticism: believes there's no way to know if God is real. Agnostics think faith, believing without proof, is foolish. They say you cannot know for sure. It's "I don't know-ism." **But** the Bible says,

"Faith is being . . . certain of what we do not see. . . . Without faith it isn't possible to please God. Those who come to God must believe that he exists" (Hebrews 11:1, 6).

Atheism: believes there is no God. End of story. The universe just happened. **But** the Bible says, "Foolish people say in their hearts, 'There is no God'" (Psalm 14:1).

Pantheism: believes God didn't make the universe; the universe *is* God. Nature is another name for God.

You're as much God as an oak tree, a beaver, or a star. **But** the Bible tells us God created things different from himself. "In the beginning, God created the heavens and the earth" (Genesis 1:1).

Pluralism: believes there are many right ways to God. People can believe whatever they want. It all leads to the same place. They say Jesus isn't the way to God. In fact, it's wrong to tell people he is. **But** Jesus made it very clear and simple, "I am the way and the truth and the life. No one comes to the Father except through me" (John 14:6).

Polytheism: believes there are many gods responsible for different parts of life. Some are more important or powerful than others. Some are evil. People can become gods. **But** God said, "I am the one and only God. . . . There is no other god" (Isaiah 46:9).

What Happened?

Adam and Eve's bad choice affected *everything!*

Death and separation from God: God is life. Sin separates us from God. Being separated from life means death—in our spirits and bodies.

Pain: We have sickness, pain, and sadness. We hurt each other. People lie, blame, get angry, and are mean. Our bodies and hearts hurt.

Hard work: We work hard just to eat and have clothes and houses.

Nature is dangerous: Thorns and thistles scratch. Snakes are poisonous. Predators kill. Bacteria cause diseases. Mosquitos bite!

The world groans: Things decay and rot. Our planet is in bad shape. "We know that all that God created has been groaning. It is in pain" (Romans 8:22).

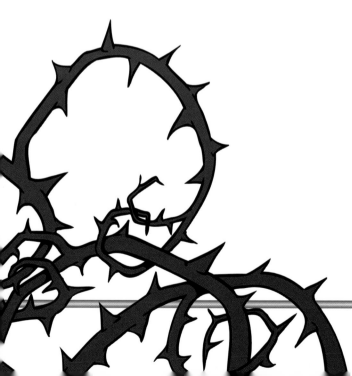

Various Religions

Beliefs About God

When you don't know someone it's easy to make up things about them. People who didn't know God came up with beliefs about him and taught them as true views of God. Does that make them true? No. The truth is always the truth no matter what we think about it. The Bible says God is truth. If we really want truth, we'll find God.

Here are some false beliefs:

Buddhism

About 2500 years ago a man believed he found *enlightenment* or true knowledge. He became *Buddha* and taught:

(1) Life is suffering. (2) We suffer because we want things. (3) To avoid suffering, stop wanting! (4) To stop wanting, have right thinking, goals, efforts, speech, behavior, actions, understanding, and meditation. This leads to life's goal, *nirvana*, where we become nothing. We have no souls. We keep being reborn into new lives until we reach nirvana.

Buddhists believe God is pure nothingness. But God is a person. He says, "I AM WHO I AM" (Exodus 3:14).

Hinduism

From a worm to a god! Hinduism says this can happen:

(1) There are many gods, but they're all *Brahman*. (2) Only *Brahman* is real—the universe isn't really here. (3) *Brahman* is the eternal soul or god. Life's goal is to realize *we* are *Brahman*. (4) We do this through living good lives. We have many! We might start as worms. If we're good worms, we might be reborn as birds. Eventually, if we're good, we're born as humans. (5) There are four *castes* or classes of people. We start at the

bottom (as laborers) and move up to priests by living each life well. Once we've been good priests, we're united with the eternal soul, *Brahman*.

Hindus believe God has no personality. But God says, "I am a God who is tender and kind. I am gracious. . . . slow to get angry. . . . faithful and full of love. I continue to show my love to thousands of people. I forgive those who do evil. . . . who refuse to obey . . . and who sin" (Exodus 34:6–7).

Islam

About 1400 years ago, a man named Mohammed said he had a revelation from God or *Allah*.

Five Beliefs: (1) There's only one God. (2) The chief angel is Gabriel. Shaitan is a fallen angel. (3) The scriptures are the Koran (Mohammed's ideas) and some parts of the Bible. (4) There are twenty-four prophets, including Jesus. Mohammed was the greatest. (5) Allah will judge the dead.

Five Duties: (1) Become a Muslim by publicly saying, "There is no god but Allah and Mohammed is his prophet." (2) Pray five times daily toward the city of Mecca. (3) Give gifts to the poor. (4) Fast in daytime during the Muslim month of Ramadan. (5) Visit the temple in Mecca. These things save you.

Muslims believe that only strict obedience to Islamic laws matters to God. But the Bible says love matters. "Suppose I can understand all the secret things of God and know everything about him. And suppose I have enough faith to move mountains. If I don't have love, I am nothing at all. Suppose I give everything I have to poor people. . . . If I don't have love, I get nothing at all" (1 Corinthians 13:2–3).

Jesus Shows Us God

Behind-the-Scenes Cause

How do we find out who God really is? We read the Bible and look at Jesus!

Why do you buy candy? Because you're hungry or just for fun? Your reason is your *motivation*, your behind-the-scenes cause. We have different motivations for what we do. Imagine having the same motivation for every single thing! God does. His one motivation is *love*.

Think about this: you're human. You can't do anything that's not human—say, make food from sunlight or breathe oxygen under water. In the same way, God is love! He can't do anything that's not loving.

Love in a Body

Picture love as a person. What would she look like? Blonde? Chubby and jolly? Stop! Love *is* a person. Love looks just like God. If you're not sure that helps, get this: God became a person like you and me. His name was Jesus Christ. He came to show us what love looks and acts like. "How did God show his love for us? He sent his one and only Son into the world" (1 John 4:9).

God sent Jesus, his Son, to live among us as a human. God is loving and unselfish. He wanted to give to us. Even with the relationship broken, God never stopped loving us. "God loved the world so much that he gave his one and only Son" (John 3:16). Jesus came to show us God. Like a lion, he is strong and fierce. He will protect us. And like a lamb, he's gentle and humble. He's the "Lamb of God [who] takes away the sin of the world" (John 1:29).

Jesus was Love in a body.

Jesus Shows Love

While Jesus lived here, people saw, touched, and heard God. Jesus was God made visible. "Christ is the exact likeness of God, who can't be seen" (Colossians 1:15). Here's what Jesus showed us. God:

Cares about our pain: Jesus healed the sick and brought dead people back to life. He cried with people and helped those in pain and trouble.

Looks after our needs: Jesus fed people and gave to the poor.

Helps us know the truth: Jesus taught about God and preached the great news of his love.

Welcomes us: Jesus welcomed all kinds of people and let them hang around him, including children, lepers, sinners, the rich, and the poor.

Is kind: A sinful woman everyone looked down on approached Jesus. He let her wash his feet with her tears and dry them with her hair. And he forgave her sins.

Read more about Jesus in the Bible's Gospels: Matthew, Mark, Luke, and John.

Jesus Is God

Here are verses that tell us Jesus is God:

God's voice from the cloud said, "This is my Son, and I love him. I am very pleased with him. Listen to him!" (Matthew 17:5).

"I and the Father are one. . . .When they look at me, they see the One who sent me. . . . If you really knew me, you would know my Father. . . . Anyone who has seen me has seen the Father" (John 10:30; 12:45; 14:7, 9).

"God was pleased to have his whole nature living in Christ . . . in human form" (Colossians 1:19; 2:9).

"The Son is the gleaming brightness of God's glory. He is the exact likeness of God's being" (Hebrews 1:3).

Jesus Saves Us

A-Mazing

Jesus helped us understand who God is again. He opened the way and brought us back to the beginning, to God's intention to be our Father!

Ever been stuck in a maze? Dead ends everywhere. No matter which way you turn or how many paths you try, you're stuck. It's frustrating and possibly frightening. Help!

Life can be like a maze. People keep looking for ways to reach God. Many, like the Buddhists, Hindus, and Muslims, think they've found it. But they've found only dead ends.

God made the way for us—he sent his Son. Jesus lived as one of us to show us what God is like by how he lived and acted. He came so we'd know he can understand us—our temptations and problems. Finally, he lived with us—to die for us!

The Way Was Death

Jesus lived to die!

Sin wrecked the relationship and still separates us from God. It puts a big dead end between us and all the paths we try to take to get to him.

"Everyone has sinned. . . . When you sin, the pay you get is death" (Romans 3:23; 6:23). Since we all sin, we all deserve to die. But God had a plan. If someone without sin was willing to die in our place to pay for our sins, God would accept that payment. He would forgive us, and we could have that great Father/child relationship with him. No more dead ends!

That's exactly what Jesus did! He lived without sin. He was innocent, but he paid for our sins by dying a horrible death on a cross. His friends put his body in a tomb, but that wasn't the end. No way! On the third day he was alive again! He reached right through all the dead ends and opened the way to relationship with God again.

Walking Through

Now instead of a dead end there's a clearly marked way that says, "To God." It's open to everyone who (1) believes Jesus is God's Son, (2) admits they're a sinner who needs forgiveness, (3) accepts that Jesus paid for their sins, (4) asks God to forgive them, be their Lord, and live in them, and (5) with God's help, lives as God wants.

Jesus is the way through the maze! We don't have to try to find God. God came to us! "Jesus answered, 'I am the way and the truth and the life. No one comes to the Father except through me'" (John 14:6). We're saved and alive forever! "But God gives you the gift of eternal life because of what Christ our Lord has done" (Romans 6:23).

A Salvation Prayer

If you haven't accepted Jesus yet and you want to be God's child, pray this prayer: "Dear God, I know I'm a sinner. I've made wrong choices and done bad things. I'm sorry. Please forgive me. I know your Son, Jesus, died for my sins. I believe you raised him from the dead, and he is Lord. I accept what he did for me. Help me trust and obey you and make right choices. Thanks for loving me, living in me, and making me your child. In Jesus' name, amen."

You're forgiven! Party time!

23

Growing with God

Begin the Adventure

Yahoo! We're back with God! Now what? Do you make the track team and stop running? No way! Making the team is the beginning! Next come the fun and the work. Being a Christian (God's child) is the same. We become a Christian and the fun begins!

Now that we have our Father/child relationship with God back, we need to start doing things his way, like Jesus did. God is now our Father who guides, teaches, protects, and watches over us as he has wanted to. And we learn how to be his children by talking to him, and trusting and obeying him.

Relationship

"Continue to work out your own salvation. . . . God is working in you" (Philippians 2:12–13). Ever try to have a relationship with someone who didn't want one? Relationships take two. God works on it with us. We get to know people by talking and sharing our hearts with them. It's the same with God. We spend time getting to know him by reading his book, meeting his other children, and talking to him in prayer.

And we obey him. Jesus said, "If you love me, you will obey what I command" (John 14:15). God wants us to obey him because he loves us. Remember, he knows everything. He knows the best way to live and what will make us happy.

God's Goal

Why does God want this relationship with us? It's the whole purpose of creation! Talk about important! God made us to love and be with. It's hard to imagine that someone would want our love so much they'd make a universe, wait hundreds of years, and die to get it! But that's

The fruit the Holy Spirit produces is love, joy, peace. It is being patient, kind . . . faithful and gentle and having control of oneself.

Galatians 5:22–23

Help Along the Way

The Bible: God gave us the Bible to help us know him. It's his love letter telling us about himself. It's also the instruction manual for a good life. When it says "Don't lie," that's because God knows lying hurts us. The Bible teaches us truth. It corrects and trains us in what's right. (See 2 Timothy 3:16–17.)

Prayer: Relationships are built through communication. We communicate with God through prayer. Prayer involves sharing our hearts with God. Also, through prayer we ask for what we and others need. God says if we come to him, he'll be glad to answer.

The Church: You're not the only Christian. You're part of a huge family! It's important to join a church, a group of God's children. In church we learn about God, grow together, and help each other. The church also helps the poor and tells others about God.

exactly what God did. He wants to care for us better than the best dad, guide and teach us more than the most knowledgeable teacher, protect us better than the greatest warrior, and encourage and cheer us on more than the best friend. That's why he made us.

As our relationship grows, we'll find almost without noticing it that we start to resemble Jesus. We become people others like to be with. We see God's fruit in our lives. "The fruit the Holy Spirit produces is love, joy, peace. It is being patient, kind . . . good. . . . faithful and gentle and having control of oneself" (Galatians 5:22–23).

Celebrate!

What Is God Like?

God can do anything. He saved his people by making a dry road through a sea!

God is the only god. In a challenge with the followers of a fake god, God's fire burned up the altar.

God is faithful. When Daniel was punished for obeying God, God kept him safe. He shut the lions' mouths.

What a Person!

Who is this God we're getting to know? In some ways he's similar to us.

What's your personality? Friendly, quiet, adventurous, studious? These qualities—your likes, attitudes, and quirks—make up your personality. You're a complicated person! Did you know God has personality? He is full of personality! And all of God's qualities, likes, attitudes, and quirks are perfect, *infinite*, and without limits. It boggles the mind!

What a Character!

Our character is the quality that guides what we do and how we live. God has great character! He is:

Good: God gives as much goodness as people can handle. He puts others first. Jesus healed the sick and fed the hungry. He even died so his enemies could be forgiven! God acts good because God is good. And he'll be good to us. Count on it!

Honest and Truthful: God is always the same, no matter what. How God acts is who God is. He is truth! He can't lie, tell part truths, say things he doesn't mean, or pretend to be someone he isn't.

Loving: Warm, fuzzy feelings. Hugs. Kind words. Acceptance. These say "love" to us. Love is treating people gently, with respect. It's wanting to be with them and wanting the best for them. God *is* love. Everything he does comes out of love—including discipline. God's love knows what's best for us.

Merciful: Remember how you're disciplined when you get in trouble? You probably deserve it. But sometimes we don't get what we deserve—we get mercy instead. Mercy is undeserved kindness, patience, and forgiveness. God knows what we've done and why. But he doesn't give us what we deserve. He's infinitely merciful. We can come to him without fear even when we've done wrong.

Perfect in Character: Look through a window on a sunny day, and you'll see smudges. The sun shows them up. God is like a pure, clean, glass window—no sun will ever show smudges on him! He's holy. That means there's nothing bad in him at all. He's perfect! Perfectly good, perfectly true, perfectly loving, perfectly merciful. There will never be the tiniest wrong in God.

All this means we can trust God. He's always the same. And he loves us. He wants to bless, care for, and be close to us. And he always acts toward us according to his character.

God is like a merciful father. He always welcomes us.

God's Character Sketch

"Lord, you are good. You are forgiving. You are full of love for all who call out to you" (Psalm 86:5).

"The Lord is good. His faithful love continues forever" (Psalm 100:5).

"The Lord . . . is kind and tender. . . . He is faithful and right in everything he does. All his rules can be trusted. . . . He is faithful and honest" (Psalm 111:4, 7–8).

"God is spirit" (John 4:24).

"The One who promised is faithful" (Hebrews 10:23).

"Every good and perfect gift is from God. It comes down from the Father. . . . He does not change like shadows that move" (James 1:17).

"God is love" (1 John 4:16).

And God said, "I have loved you with a love that lasts forever. I have kept on loving you with faithful love" (Jeremiah 31:3).

God Is Faithful

Unchanging God

God sounds great! But what does that mean for us? Lots!

Imagine that one day gravity quits! You'd have to grab something quick, or you'd float away! Without gravity you'd never come back to Earth. But don't worry, you can count on gravity. Wherever there's a large mass, like Earth, there's gravity. Always. We build our lives around the fact that gravity will keep doing its thing.

God *made* gravity! He's way more consistent than it is. "I am the Lord. I do not change" (Malachi 3:6). "[The heavens] will pass away. But you remain" (Hebrews 1:11). God never changes. We can build our lives around *that* fact. God's character will always be God's character. More than gravity, God is always the same.

Trustworthy, Faithful God

We can trust someone when we know their character and that they care about us and can help us. We know God's character and love for us means he'll always act with our best in mind. We can trust him. We don't even have to think about it! He's *trustworthy!* We can trust God with our lives because we know his

way is the best way and will make our lives better.

Once we trust someone, we need to know he can do what we're trusting him for. We need to know that when he says he'll do something, he will, no question. God will. He's *faithful*. We can put our faith in God and rely on him to do what he said he would do as our Father: look after us and help us grow.

God spoke to Moses through the burning bush. Moses trusted God to lead him.

Noah obeyed God even when he didn't understand. And God saved him.

Timeless Love

Love isn't just touchy-feely warm fuzzies. God's love is strong. He's there for the long haul. He cares who you are now and who you'll become. He sees your whole life and knows how to make you into the best person you can be. He doesn't pop into your life for a day, give an order, then take off for months. No way! He's with you all the time. He cares about every part of your character and life. He wants you to be a loving, respected person and, later, have a good job, strong friend-ships, and a solid, loving marriage.

All that takes a God who's always the same, always faithful, who cares about both the details *and* the big picture. That's exactly who God is! We can count on his love! Absolutely.

Faith Test

God knows exactly what he's doing. Sometimes when bad things happen, it doesn't *feel* like God loves us. Maybe we move to a school where we can't find friends. It's hard to feel God's love. What's going on?

Look at the big picture. What's more important—our relationship with God and his plan for our lives and growth, or a quick fix? Sometimes, for our sakes, God lets things happen because he knows what we need to become the best possible us. "Your troubles have come in order to prove that your faith is real. It is worth more than gold" (1 Peter 1:7). No matter what, one thing never changes: God loves us. Even though we may not understand what is happening to us, God is working out everything for our good. That's as solid as rock, as certain as gravity.

Great Big God

God is so big that we've barely begun to find out who he is in this book. No matter how much we get to know him, there's always more to learn. We'll never get bored with God as our Father and friend!

Q Who created God?

A No one created God—he has always existed. We can't understand this because everything that we know has a beginning or an end. Each day has a morning and night; basketball games have an opening tip-off and a final buzzer; people are born, and they die. But God has no beginning or end. He always was and always will be.

Q How and why did God create the world?

JASON'S IMAGINATION

A Whenever we make something, like a craft, a drawing, or a sand castle, we have to start with special materials, like clay, string, glue, paper, crayons, and sand. We can't even imagine creating something out of nothing—by just saying the words and making it appear. But God is so powerful that he can do what is impossible for us. That includes making anything he wants, even creating things from nothing. That's what it means to be God—he can do anything.

God created the world and everything in it because he enjoys making things, and he wanted to be with us.

God created people because he wanted to have friends, men and women, boys and girls, with whom he could share his love. He created the world for them to live in and enjoy.

Q How does God make the sun and moon go up and down?

A God made powerful laws to govern the universe. These laws control the movements of the sun, moon, earth, and other planets and stars. For example, one law called "gravity" draws objects toward each other. Other natural laws control the weather. Many forces determine whether the day will be sunny or cloudy, warm or cold, such as the heat from the sun, the currents in the ocean, the wind, and many others. God set up the rules that make all these forces work together. And because God controls the entire universe, he can interrupt the laws if he

wants to—bring rain to dry land or bright sunshine to flooded areas. How powerful God must be to control all that!

Q Would God send nice people to hell if they are not Christians?

A Compared to each other, some people are nice and some are

mean. But compared to God, all people are not very good. All people need to be forgiven for their sins, not just "mean people." To be fair, God has to punish sin. God doesn't want to send anyone to hell. That's why he sent Jesus—to pay the penalty for our sins by dying on the cross. But, unfortunately, not all people are willing to admit that they sin and ask for forgiveness. They don't accept the payment of Jesus' death for them. So God lets them experience the result of their choice.

Adapted from *101 Questions Children Ask About God*, Tyndale House Publishers, Inc., 1992. Used by permission.

Put It All Together

Big Dreams

What would make you the happiest kid in the world? Having scientists prove that eating junk food is good for you? Having your own plane to fly all around the world? Having a huge toy store to share with your friends? What is the greatest blessing you could have? The true happiness key—the blessing that will last forever and fill you to-the-brim full of joy—is what this book is all about: a relationship with the God who made and loves you! With God by your side, life can't get any better!

Our Hero

We all have heroes: movie stars, athletes, musicians. Imagine meeting your hero and hanging out with him or her! What a privilege!

God is the greatest hero of all. Being able to hang out with and get to know him is the greatest privilege of all. Relationship with him isn't a requirement or something we ought to do. It's an awesome chance to know the greatest hero of all time. God has invited us not just to hang out with him for a short time, but to be with him always! Wow! Talk about a privilege!

God knows us inside and out, and he loves us. He enjoys spending time with us.

When we started this book, we looked at the stars and saw God in what he made. We learned about who he is by looking at what he made and what the Bible said. Now we're setting out on a journey to get to know him the best possible way: personally! When we take God up on his invitation, we'll find he becomes more and more real to us.

Let's seek this incredible God and have the greatest happiness!